Nuclear Shadows of Palm Trees

Nikolai Garcia

a DSTL arts publication

Nuclear Shadows of Palm Trees

a DSTL Arts publication

The work in this book was written by Nikolai Garcia, a participant in DSTL Arts's Arts Mentorship Program, and first printed in August, 2019 by DSTL Arts publishing in Los Angeles, CA, U.S.A.

Cover Design: Luis Antonio Pichardo

Original Cover Image/Photograph: Monica Serrano
(follow on Instagram using @jvm_m86)

Book Design: Luis Antonio Pichardo

ISBN: 978-1-946081-31-5

10 9 8 7 6 5 4 3 2 1

www.DSTLArts.org

Los Angeles, CA

content:

"You're gonna be one of those L.A. poets"

Dedicated to the memory of Carol Lem
(1944-2012)
Poet, Teacher, Buddhist, Chinese Chicana

A Long Drive

Wake up from a dream you can't remember.
Your heart is a compass.
It points north, you obey.

Climb into an old car painted
by heat and smog. You fumble
with a pack of cigarettes
before turning on
the engine. Soon,
hands and sweat are attached
to the steering wheel
and you're on
the I-5 to Sacramento.

Cruise through the San Fernando Valley:
Think about a woman;
the affection in her voice;
taste the galaxy on her ears;
the dead leaves in her eyes.

Remember a couple of days,
as if
they were weeks.
Remember one night,
as if
it never ended.

Somewhere
in the San Joaquin Valley,
the sun is an oppressor,
and the smells
of grapes, asparagus, and apricots become
a permanent salad in the air.
Pull your car over,
vomit on the side
of the road.

Tell your heart it's an idiot;
turn the car around,
start driving
back to Los Angeles.

Somewhere
up north, a little girl
is happy to have a mother
to help with
math homework, and love
only her—if nobody else.
For you, there

are only miles ahead
on an interstate built
into darkness, and songs
of lost love coming
from the oldies station.

Confessional Poem #1

Spent a majority
of childhood on 41st street:
In a big
white and red house, surrounded
by giant palm trees and Avalon
Gangsta Crips—both of whom
played with clouds. There

were brown-eyed dobermans and a Pink
Panther ice-cream truck. Across
the street lived Marisol
Torres—blond hair, blue eyes—she
was the whitest Mexican
I ever knew. One night,

a cousin was shot
dead at the corner
store. He had a long Spanish name
I never learned

how to spell. He belonged
to a local gang and was
killed
by the local rivals. There,

blood everywhere. I walked
past it on my way
to school. That day I learned
blood has two
colors: the bright, radish-red
when leaving your body;
and the rusty
brownish-red after drying
on concrete.

Portrait of A Homeless Youth with Lizard

Gabriel woke
up near the Hollywood
Freeway, sleeping
on his side, under
a brush and smog. As the sun
rose from the east, he noticed
a creature nestled between
the earth and his belly.

Gabriel slowly moved
his hand offering it
to the creature. It wrapped
around Gabriel's hand, making
him smile.

Gabriel
named the lizard, Hope, placing

it on his shoulder. Wherever
Gabriel went, Hope went. Whenever
Gabriel ate, Hope ate. Whenever
Gabriel slept, Hope slept.

When people asked where
he found his lizard, Gabriel
liked to say, "I didn't find
Hope; Hope found
me."

Everyone is Flirting with the New Waitress

Even the drunks going
six days straight without
a shower, and the crack
addicts going six hours straight
without a hit, are on
their best behavior.

I just want
my coffee.

Men dressed in wrinkles
and white hair, freshly
cashed SSI checks, flash
bills around like rich
bankers.

I just want

my bacon and egg sandwich.

Middle-aged White men,
who have always
noticed the accent
of the city, but never spoke
a word of Spanish in their lives,
trip over their tongues
saying, "O-la," and,
"bue-knows dios."

I just want
my second cup of coffee.

Their shiny words slip
off her apron and none
of the compliments make it
to her ears as
she rushes back and forth
from the kitchen, balancing
plates of pancakes, eggs,
sausages and hash browns.

But still they try—these men
of Skid Row—whom I believed
given up on life
and, therefore, love.
But with every chance they get
they try

to look in her eyes.

I just want
my exact change (and
her phone number).

Walking Around Skid Row

After Nikki Giovanni

walking down Main
street
or Spring street do you ever wonder
was it any better
before the lofts arrived
do you ever stop and stare at a man,
face covered with smog and misery,
lying on the asphalt
as a hipster walks their dog
beside him (nothing bad
around us
as long as we keep
moving)

did you ever wonder
what home was like
before they gave it rules
and regulations

so they could attach applications,
waiting lists, and criminal records
to it
do you want to know what will happen
if you get your own place
if someone
will love you

ever look west,
when they sun will let you,
past the dealers on the corner
past the carts of hot dogs hugged
by bacon
and think maybe
there's a place for you
to lay head on pillow
and finally dream

and, tell me, have you ever
wondered what it would be like
if there were no such things
as landlords
would you walk these buildings
looking for an apartment
and see that you could get one
easily

ever wonder what
would happen if the housing authority

blew up
would anyone deny housing
at any SRO buildings like
the Sanborn, the Dewey,
the Abbey apartments

have you realized yet that skid row will never
be the same and that
the galleries and the hipsters are here to stay
to join the mentally ill and liquor stores
and cars vroooooming down the wrong side
of a one-way street
and everybody hustling under the same sun,
some selling art, others fruit, others drugs
or begging for change

everybody has to
pay rent on
the first

Suicide Prevention Training

The lead psychologist talked
about warning signs and
what to do,
but all I could
think of was a text
I received two months ago:
> *I'm going to kill myself...*
I don't want to be here anymore.

I was at work and didn't
look at my phone
when it beeped. And when I
finally saw the message,
I almost fell
into the screen.

I dialed her number,
the line just rang,
and rang,

and rang...

For weeks, we had been texting
late at night.
She—mostly bored, and
me—mostly drunk.
But, somewhere, in between
our words,
a trust had been born.

When she finally answered,
her voice reached
inside of me
softly, like doves
landing on your shoulder.

Through the training we learned
most who attempt suicide
do not want to die;
they just want the pain
to stop. Sometimes,
I'll look at my phone screen
and wonder which
one of us had been feeling
the most pain.

An L.A. Storm

Clouds gather
en masse. Raindrops become
heavier than heaven giving
Los Angeles a storm.

Freeways flooded.
There's no escape
from water; life—
we are drenched.

With filth and vermin
down the gutters, the city
gives its permission for a thousand
flowers to blossom.

Looking at the sky, rain—
clouds that linger, can be
mistaken for a fire's
smoke.

Downtown L.A. Bar at Noon

Beer spilling, vodka
splashing, whiskey dreams
deferred. Inside this
darkness, Bukowski's ghost
hovers next to shadows
slouching on barstools.

Dust gathers on top-shelf
bottles while melancholy
music plays on the juke
box, sadder than a wet one
dollar tip that lays
on the counter, untouched.

Whenever the front door opens,
and sunlight sneaks in, old
souls momentarily regain

the consciousness they let
drown in pints of Guinness.

Wanda Coleman's Roar

I don't smoke weed, I smoke palm
trees. I rise into clouds like

the 110-105 interchange. I take back
airspace from a LAPD chopper, examining

freeways; concrete ribbons, anchoring our smog
and beaches to the West Coast. Each night

I dream about Wanda Coleman.
She tells me one day I'll be

as big as the Watts Towers. She says,
point your finger in any direction, eventually

you'll hit a freeway. Her laugh, a roar.
I marvel at how Manchester Ave. creeps

into Firestone Blvd. I promise myself

when the freeways begin to crumble,

and the city drifts into the Pacific,
I will stand watch. When the final palm

tree goes up in flames, Wanda
Coleman's roar will be the last thing

I want to hear.

I Can't Even

"La tristesse durera toujours"

I met her for the first
time near the Pacific
Ocean; now I dream
dead mermaids, wash up
on the shore.

Oftentimes, I think
about van Gogh's final
painting; obviously,
she got me feeling
some type of way.

I have a room
in my house where
it rains all day. This
is the reason why
my shirts are always wet.

I don't want to hold on
to this grudge. But
everywhere—everything—is painted
with memory.

Inheritance

On her only day
off from work, my mother rises
from her bed while the moon
and sun switch shifts.

She wakes
her only daughter; with arms
full of flowers, they travel
five miles to my father's grave.

Dad was a good
provider to his children; worked
every damn day of his life. But, to my
mother, he was not faithful.

I found it hard to
understand why she feels
compelled to honor this ritual years
after my dad paid any bills.

One day, I found myself
writing poem
after poem to a woman
that was gone and wondered
if I inherited the same
kind of madness.

I look through
my journal and see
a graveyard I built
myself with pen and ink.
I don't want to leave
her flowers anymore.

The Wedding

I was at a wedding.
At a villa—somewhere in Napa
Valley—miles of vineyards,
a veranda full of guests.

To my left,
a groom in a cream tuxedo. Teary
-eyed, smiling, he sat alone
at a long table full of gifts
wrapped in shiny paper and big bows,
surrounding a five-layer cake.

On my right,
a crowd of women stood
behind the bride. One,
in black shoes, black dress,
fishnet stockings, a shadow
against the sun.

Suddenly, a ball of white
flew over the bride's head
landing in the dark
figure's hands; white roses
and calla lilies clashing
with neon pink nails.

An applause filled the air,
as she stepped towards me.
Red-faced as a glass of wine,
she leaned into my ear whispering,
"I'm the only one here
with fishnets."

At that moment, I awoke
startled,
there was no wedding; only
the smell of rotting
grapes in the air.

One-Night Stand

A stranger came home with me one night.
I found her while wandering down
Fourth Street, after drifting away from my
friends. She was sitting alone at a bus-stop,
after getting kicked out of a bar. I asked
if she knew the bus schedule. She shook
her head, reached into her jacket, and
offered me her flask. I took a swig,
gave it back, and we both started walking.
We talked about growing up in South Central; punk bands
we liked; and being single,
while raising children with people
who no longer loved us. By the time
we got to the train
station, she told me her entire life
story, but we missed the last train heading south. When we
finally made it to my place, we fell
on the bed--tired from life. That night,
with the help of the moon,

I contemplated the curls in her hair
and her burnt cinnamon skin. I stayed
awake all night wondering if she
would reach over and murder me.

Stoppage of Play

The threat of nuclear
war has caused a delayed
game at Dodger Stadium.

Thousands
of loyal fans remain
in their seats pecking
at smart phones.

On the jumbo screen,
an announcement
from the President: "America
first," he says. The crowd
goes wild.

Meanwhile,
in Congress, bobbleheads
nod in approval.

Not even the silly
hopes for a World
Series will remain
at Chavez Ravine.

Nuclear shadows of palm
trees will be
the only evidence
of where a city
once stood.

While Sitting On the Tijuana Border

I sit under
the night; a cigarette
between my lips. I think
of someone as I
glance at the sky
letting the ghost inside
my mouth escape,
rise, disappear.

A few feet
away, sitting
on a curb, a drunk
yells out sad
rancheras at the moon.
The only difference
between us is how
we sing our songs.

Instructions on How to Decorate My Grave on Día de los Muertos

For Monica Serrano

Start by making a mixtape.
Title it, "Depression Soundtrack."
(Don't forget to bring a tape player
so we can listen while you work).
Place two palm fronds at the top
corners of my headstone
for that California aesthetic.
Remember, I was diabetic
so substitute sugar skulls
with a head of lettuce. Draw a face on it.
Stand above my grave, cradling
two dozen orange and yellow
marigolds. Slowly drop them.
Where they fall is where they belong.

Remember something funny I said and leave
a pint of Jameson—none of that cheap whiskey.
Walk away
and don't think of me for eleven months.

Confessional Poem #3

After Michael Robbins

I am 31 with cartoon characters on my shirts.
A young sloth. Sometimes I mistake
my own arm for a branch and fall.
You shouldn't have taken me as a pet.
We never should have met.

Every morning, when I wake,
I think about revolution.
Every night, I think of a woman.
She was fine with her living arrangement
until the day she met me.

Me gusta el reggae y tambien el punk.
I will buy you a few beers, but I like to spend
the least amount of money to get drunk.
Sometimes, when I wake and it's raining,
I wonder if any raindrops have touched you.

I didn't want to take things slow
because I was in the Amazon and wanted to go.
I will lick the raindrops off your face.
Does that sound dumb?
You can name the time and the place.

No More Poems About L.A.

No more Griffith Park or L.A. Zoo
No more Crenshaw Blvd. or MLK parade
No more intersection of Florence & Normandie

No more freeway worship or images of palm trees
No more starless skies or kissing on the beach
No more three-dollar Lyft rides from Joe's Pizza to Hank's
Bar

No more lowriders sleep-walking down Whittier
No more girls with cat-eyes and big-hoop earrings
No more sitting at the park waiting for you

No more overdue books at Central Library
No more references to Bukowski
No more cold blood on hot concrete

No more fried chicken with a side of chow mein
No more still-life paintings of tacos

No more odes to Jonathan Gold

No more baseball in October
No more loud graffiti on an overpass sign
No more smog romanticism or similes for traffic

It's time to burn down the Hollywood sign
It's time to pack my things and go.

Acknowledgements

Many thanks to the editors of the following literary journals, periodicals and anthologies in which these poems, some in different forms, first appeared:

Chaparral: "Confessional Poem #1" and "While Sitting On the Tijuana Border"

The Coiled Serpent: Poets Arising from the Cultural Quakes and Shifts of Los Angeles: "A Long Drive"

Dryland: "I Can't Even"

Statement: "Everyone Is Flirting with the New Waitress" and "Confessional Poem #3"

Spectrum: "Stoppage of Play"

Brooklyn & Boyle: "Walking Around Skid Row"

Conchas y Café Zine (DSTL Arts): "Downtown L.A. Bar at Noon," and "No More Poems About L.A."

The Arsonist: "Inheritance"

About the Poet

Nikolai Garcia is all-city L.A. He grew up in South Central Los Angeles; graduated from Birmingham High School in *The Valley*; went to East L.A. College (where he studied Journalism and Creative Writing under Jean Stapleton and Carol Lem, respectively); spent 12 years working in Skid Row; currently works in East Hollywood, and sleeps in Compton.

He has been published in the anthologies, *The Coiled Serpent*, (Tia Chucha Press), *Extreme* (Vagabond Books), and in various literary journals. He is currently Assistant Editor for *Dryland*. This is his first chapbook.

This publication was produced by DSTL Arts.

DSTL Arts is a nonprofit arts mentorship organization that inspires, teaches, and hires emerging artists from underserved communities.

To learn more about DSTL Arts, visit online at:

DSTLArts.org

 @DSTLArts
 /DSTLArts

CPSIA information can be obtained
at www.ICGtesting.com
Printed in the USA
LVHW040013060123
736517LV00009B/595